THIS JOURNAL

BELONGS TO:

O———————————O

DATE: / /

TODAY I AM THANKFUL FOR

A MOMENT TO REMEMBER

MY THOUGHTS ON TODAY

GOAL FOR TOMORROW

DATE: / /

TODAY I AM THANKFUL FOR

A MOMENT TO REMEMBER

MY THOUGHTS ON TODAY

GOAL FOR TOMORROW

DATE: / /

TODAY I AM THANKFUL FOR

A MOMENT TO REMEMBER

MY THOUGHTS ON TODAY

GOAL FOR TOMORROW

DATE: / /

TODAY I AM THANKFUL FOR

A MOMENT TO REMEMBER

MY THOUGHTS ON TODAY

GOAL FOR TOMORROW

DATE: / /

TODAY I AM THANKFUL FOR

A MOMENT TO REMEMBER

MY THOUGHTS ON TODAY

GOAL FOR TOMORROW

DATE: / /

TODAY I AM THANKFUL FOR

A MOMENT TO REMEMBER

MY THOUGHTS ON TODAY

GOAL FOR TOMORROW

DATE: / /

TODAY I AM THANKFUL FOR

A MOMENT TO REMEMBER

MY THOUGHTS ON TODAY

GOAL FOR TOMORROW

DATE: / /

TODAY I AM THANKFUL FOR

A MOMENT TO REMEMBER

MY THOUGHTS ON TODAY

GOAL FOR TOMORROW

DATE: / /

TODAY I AM THANKFUL FOR

A MOMENT TO REMEMBER

MY THOUGHTS ON TODAY

GOAL FOR TOMORROW

DATE: /   /

TODAY I AM THANKFUL FOR

A MOMENT TO REMEMBER

MY THOUGHTS ON TODAY

GOAL FOR TOMORROW

DATE: / /

TODAY I AM THANKFUL FOR

A MOMENT TO REMEMBER

MY THOUGHTS ON TODAY

GOAL FOR TOMORROW

DATE: / /

TODAY I AM THANKFUL FOR

A MOMENT TO REMEMBER

MY THOUGHTS ON TODAY

GOAL FOR TOMORROW

DATE: / /

TODAY I AM THANKFUL FOR

A MOMENT TO REMEMBER

MY THOUGHTS ON TODAY

GOAL FOR TOMORROW

DATE: / /

TODAY I AM THANKFUL FOR

A MOMENT TO REMEMBER

MY THOUGHTS ON TODAY

GOAL FOR TOMORROW

DATE: /   /

TODAY I AM THANKFUL FOR

A MOMENT TO REMEMBER

MY THOUGHTS ON TODAY

GOAL FOR TOMORROW

DATE: / /

TODAY I AM THANKFUL FOR

A MOMENT TO REMEMBER

MY THOUGHTS ON TODAY

GOAL FOR TOMORROW

DATE: / /

TODAY I AM THANKFUL FOR

A MOMENT TO REMEMBER

MY THOUGHTS ON TODAY

GOAL FOR TOMORROW

DATE: / /

TODAY I AM THANKFUL FOR

A MOMENT TO REMEMBER

MY THOUGHTS ON TODAY

GOAL FOR TOMORROW

DATE: / /

TODAY I AM THANKFUL FOR

A MOMENT TO REMEMBER

MY THOUGHTS ON TODAY

GOAL FOR TOMORROW

DATE: / /

TODAY I AM THANKFUL FOR

A MOMENT TO REMEMBER

MY THOUGHTS ON TODAY

GOAL FOR TOMORROW

DATE: / /

TODAY I AM THANKFUL FOR

A MOMENT TO REMEMBER

MY THOUGHTS ON TODAY

GOAL FOR TOMORROW

DATE: / /

TODAY I AM THANKFUL FOR

A MOMENT TO REMEMBER

MY THOUGHTS ON TODAY

GOAL FOR TOMORROW

DATE: / /

TODAY I AM THANKFUL FOR

A MOMENT TO REMEMBER

MY THOUGHTS ON TODAY

GOAL FOR TOMORROW

DATE: / /

TODAY I AM THANKFUL FOR

A MOMENT TO REMEMBER

MY THOUGHTS ON TODAY

GOAL FOR TOMORROW

DATE: / /

TODAY I AM THANKFUL FOR

A MOMENT TO REMEMBER

MY THOUGHTS ON TODAY

GOAL FOR TOMORROW

DATE: / /

TODAY I AM THANKFUL FOR

A MOMENT TO REMEMBER

MY THOUGHTS ON TODAY

GOAL FOR TOMORROW

DATE: / /

TODAY I AM THANKFUL FOR

A MOMENT TO REMEMBER

MY THOUGHTS ON TODAY

GOAL FOR TOMORROW

DATE: /   /

TODAY I AM THANKFUL FOR

A MOMENT TO REMEMBER

MY THOUGHTS ON TODAY

GOAL FOR TOMORROW

DATE: /   /

TODAY I AM THANKFUL FOR

A MOMENT TO REMEMBER

MY THOUGHTS ON TODAY

GOAL FOR TOMORROW

DATE: / /

TODAY I AM THANKFUL FOR

A MOMENT TO REMEMBER

MY THOUGHTS ON TODAY

GOAL FOR TOMORROW

DATE: / /

TODAY I AM THANKFUL FOR

A MOMENT TO REMEMBER

MY THOUGHTS ON TODAY

GOAL FOR TOMORROW

DATE: / /

TODAY I AM THANKFUL FOR

A MOMENT TO REMEMBER

MY THOUGHTS ON TODAY

GOAL FOR TOMORROW

DATE: / /

TODAY I AM THANKFUL FOR

A MOMENT TO REMEMBER

MY THOUGHTS ON TODAY

GOAL FOR TOMORROW

DATE: / /

TODAY I AM THANKFUL FOR

A MOMENT TO REMEMBER

MY THOUGHTS ON TODAY

GOAL FOR TOMORROW

DATE: / /

TODAY I AM THANKFUL FOR

A MOMENT TO REMEMBER

MY THOUGHTS ON TODAY

GOAL FOR TOMORROW

DATE: / /

TODAY I AM THANKFUL FOR

A MOMENT TO REMEMBER

MY THOUGHTS ON TODAY

GOAL FOR TOMORROW

DATE: / /

TODAY I AM THANKFUL FOR

A MOMENT TO REMEMBER

MY THOUGHTS ON TODAY

GOAL FOR TOMORROW

DATE: / /

TODAY I AM THANKFUL FOR

A MOMENT TO REMEMBER

MY THOUGHTS ON TODAY

GOAL FOR TOMORROW

DATE: / /

TODAY I AM THANKFUL FOR

A MOMENT TO REMEMBER

MY THOUGHTS ON TODAY

GOAL FOR TOMORROW

DATE: / /

TODAY I AM THANKFUL FOR

A MOMENT TO REMEMBER

MY THOUGHTS ON TODAY

GOAL FOR TOMORROW

DATE: /   /

TODAY I AM THANKFUL FOR

A MOMENT TO REMEMBER

MY THOUGHTS ON TODAY

GOAL FOR TOMORROW

DATE: / /

TODAY I AM THANKFUL FOR

A MOMENT TO REMEMBER

MY THOUGHTS ON TODAY

GOAL FOR TOMORROW

DATE: / /

TODAY I AM THANKFUL FOR

A MOMENT TO REMEMBER

MY THOUGHTS ON TODAY

GOAL FOR TOMORROW

DATE: / /

TODAY I AM THANKFUL FOR

A MOMENT TO REMEMBER

MY THOUGHTS ON TODAY

GOAL FOR TOMORROW

DATE: / /

TODAY I AM THANKFUL FOR

A MOMENT TO REMEMBER

MY THOUGHTS ON TODAY

GOAL FOR TOMORROW

DATE: / /

TODAY I AM THANKFUL FOR

A MOMENT TO REMEMBER

MY THOUGHTS ON TODAY

GOAL FOR TOMORROW

DATE: / /

TODAY I AM THANKFUL FOR

A MOMENT TO REMEMBER

MY THOUGHTS ON TODAY

GOAL FOR TOMORROW

DATE: / /

TODAY I AM THANKFUL FOR

A MOMENT TO REMEMBER

MY THOUGHTS ON TODAY

GOAL FOR TOMORROW

DATE: / /

TODAY I AM THANKFUL FOR

A MOMENT TO REMEMBER

MY THOUGHTS ON TODAY

GOAL FOR TOMORROW

DATE: / /

TODAY I AM THANKFUL FOR

A MOMENT TO REMEMBER

MY THOUGHTS ON TODAY

GOAL FOR TOMORROW

DATE: /   /

TODAY I AM THANKFUL FOR

A MOMENT TO REMEMBER

MY THOUGHTS ON TODAY

GOAL FOR TOMORROW

DATE: /   /

TODAY I AM THANKFUL FOR

A MOMENT TO REMEMBER

MY THOUGHTS ON TODAY

GOAL FOR TOMORROW

DATE: / /

TODAY I AM THANKFUL FOR

A MOMENT TO REMEMBER

MY THOUGHTS ON TODAY

GOAL FOR TOMORROW

DATE: / /

TODAY I AM THANKFUL FOR

A MOMENT TO REMEMBER

MY THOUGHTS ON TODAY

GOAL FOR TOMORROW

DATE: / /

TODAY I AM THANKFUL FOR

A MOMENT TO REMEMBER

MY THOUGHTS ON TODAY

GOAL FOR TOMORROW

DATE: / /

TODAY I AM THANKFUL FOR

A MOMENT TO REMEMBER

MY THOUGHTS ON TODAY

GOAL FOR TOMORROW

DATE: / /

TODAY I AM THANKFUL FOR

A MOMENT TO REMEMBER

MY THOUGHTS ON TODAY

GOAL FOR TOMORROW

DATE: / /

TODAY I AM THANKFUL FOR

A MOMENT TO REMEMBER

MY THOUGHTS ON TODAY

GOAL FOR TOMORROW

DATE: / /

TODAY I AM THANKFUL FOR

A MOMENT TO REMEMBER

MY THOUGHTS ON TODAY

GOAL FOR TOMORROW

DATE: / /

TODAY I AM THANKFUL FOR

A MOMENT TO REMEMBER

MY THOUGHTS ON TODAY

GOAL FOR TOMORROW

DATE: / /

TODAY I AM THANKFUL FOR

A MOMENT TO REMEMBER

MY THOUGHTS ON TODAY

GOAL FOR TOMORROW

DATE: / /

TODAY I AM THANKFUL FOR

A MOMENT TO REMEMBER

MY THOUGHTS ON TODAY

GOAL FOR TOMORROW

DATE: /   /

TODAY I AM THANKFUL FOR

A MOMENT TO REMEMBER

MY THOUGHTS ON TODAY

GOAL FOR TOMORROW

DATE: / /

TODAY I AM THANKFUL FOR

A MOMENT TO REMEMBER

MY THOUGHTS ON TODAY

GOAL FOR TOMORROW

DATE: / /

TODAY I AM THANKFUL FOR

A MOMENT TO REMEMBER

MY THOUGHTS ON TODAY

GOAL FOR TOMORROW

DATE: / /

TODAY I AM THANKFUL FOR

A MOMENT TO REMEMBER

MY THOUGHTS ON TODAY

GOAL FOR TOMORROW

DATE: / /

TODAY I AM THANKFUL FOR

A MOMENT TO REMEMBER

MY THOUGHTS ON TODAY

GOAL FOR TOMORROW

DATE: / /

TODAY I AM THANKFUL FOR

A MOMENT TO REMEMBER

MY THOUGHTS ON TODAY

GOAL FOR TOMORROW

DATE: / /

TODAY I AM THANKFUL FOR

A MOMENT TO REMEMBER

MY THOUGHTS ON TODAY

GOAL FOR TOMORROW

DATE: / /

TODAY I AM THANKFUL FOR

A MOMENT TO REMEMBER

MY THOUGHTS ON TODAY

GOAL FOR TOMORROW

DATE: / /

TODAY I AM THANKFUL FOR

A MOMENT TO REMEMBER

MY THOUGHTS ON TODAY

GOAL FOR TOMORROW

DATE: / /

TODAY I AM THANKFUL FOR

A MOMENT TO REMEMBER

MY THOUGHTS ON TODAY

GOAL FOR TOMORROW

DATE: / /

TODAY I AM THANKFUL FOR

A MOMENT TO REMEMBER

MY THOUGHTS ON TODAY

GOAL FOR TOMORROW

DATE: / /

TODAY I AM THANKFUL FOR

A MOMENT TO REMEMBER

MY THOUGHTS ON TODAY

GOAL FOR TOMORROW

DATE: / /

TODAY I AM THANKFUL FOR

A MOMENT TO REMEMBER

MY THOUGHTS ON TODAY

GOAL FOR TOMORROW

DATE: / /

TODAY I AM THANKFUL FOR

A MOMENT TO REMEMBER

MY THOUGHTS ON TODAY

GOAL FOR TOMORROW

DATE: / /

TODAY I AM THANKFUL FOR

A MOMENT TO REMEMBER

MY THOUGHTS ON TODAY

GOAL FOR TOMORROW

DATE: / /

TODAY I AM THANKFUL FOR

A MOMENT TO REMEMBER

MY THOUGHTS ON TODAY

GOAL FOR TOMORROW

DATE: / /

TODAY I AM THANKFUL FOR

A MOMENT TO REMEMBER

MY THOUGHTS ON TODAY

GOAL FOR TOMORROW

DATE: / /

TODAY I AM THANKFUL FOR

A MOMENT TO REMEMBER

MY THOUGHTS ON TODAY

GOAL FOR TOMORROW

DATE: / /

TODAY I AM THANKFUL FOR

A MOMENT TO REMEMBER

MY THOUGHTS ON TODAY

GOAL FOR TOMORROW

DATE: / /

TODAY I AM THANKFUL FOR

A MOMENT TO REMEMBER

MY THOUGHTS ON TODAY

GOAL FOR TOMORROW

DATE: / /

--- TODAY I AM THANKFUL FOR ---

--- A MOMENT TO REMEMBER ---

--- MY THOUGHTS ON TODAY ---

--- GOAL FOR TOMORROW ---

DATE: / /

TODAY I AM THANKFUL FOR

A MOMENT TO REMEMBER

MY THOUGHTS ON TODAY

GOAL FOR TOMORROW

DATE: / /

TODAY I AM THANKFUL FOR

A MOMENT TO REMEMBER

MY THOUGHTS ON TODAY

GOAL FOR TOMORROW

DATE: / /

TODAY I AM THANKFUL FOR

A MOMENT TO REMEMBER

MY THOUGHTS ON TODAY

GOAL FOR TOMORROW

DATE: / /

TODAY I AM THANKFUL FOR

A MOMENT TO REMEMBER

MY THOUGHTS ON TODAY

GOAL FOR TOMORROW

DATE: / /

TODAY I AM THANKFUL FOR

A MOMENT TO REMEMBER

MY THOUGHTS ON TODAY

GOAL FOR TOMORROW

DATE: / /

TODAY I AM THANKFUL FOR

A MOMENT TO REMEMBER

MY THOUGHTS ON TODAY

GOAL FOR TOMORROW

DATE: / /

TODAY I AM THANKFUL FOR

A MOMENT TO REMEMBER

MY THOUGHTS ON TODAY

GOAL FOR TOMORROW

DATE: / /

TODAY I AM THANKFUL FOR

A MOMENT TO REMEMBER

MY THOUGHTS ON TODAY

GOAL FOR TOMORROW

DATE: / /

---- TODAY I AM THANKFUL FOR ----

---- A MOMENT TO REMEMBER ----

---- MY THOUGHTS ON TODAY ----

---- GOAL FOR TOMORROW ----

DATE: / /

TODAY I AM THANKFUL FOR

A MOMENT TO REMEMBER

MY THOUGHTS ON TODAY

GOAL FOR TOMORROW

DATE: / /

TODAY I AM THANKFUL FOR

A MOMENT TO REMEMBER

MY THOUGHTS ON TODAY

GOAL FOR TOMORROW

DATE: /   /

TODAY I AM THANKFUL FOR

A MOMENT TO REMEMBER

MY THOUGHTS ON TODAY

GOAL FOR TOMORROW

DATE: / /

TODAY I AM THANKFUL FOR

A MOMENT TO REMEMBER

MY THOUGHTS ON TODAY

GOAL FOR TOMORROW

DATE: / /

TODAY I AM THANKFUL FOR

A MOMENT TO REMEMBER

MY THOUGHTS ON TODAY

GOAL FOR TOMORROW

DATE: / /

TODAY I AM THANKFUL FOR

A MOMENT TO REMEMBER

MY THOUGHTS ON TODAY

GOAL FOR TOMORROW

DATE: / /

TODAY I AM THANKFUL FOR

A MOMENT TO REMEMBER

MY THOUGHTS ON TODAY

GOAL FOR TOMORROW

DATE: / /

TODAY I AM THANKFUL FOR

A MOMENT TO REMEMBER

MY THOUGHTS ON TODAY

GOAL FOR TOMORROW

DATE: /   /

TODAY I AM THANKFUL FOR

A MOMENT TO REMEMBER

MY THOUGHTS ON TODAY

GOAL FOR TOMORROW

DATE: / /

TODAY I AM THANKFUL FOR

A MOMENT TO REMEMBER

MY THOUGHTS ON TODAY

GOAL FOR TOMORROW

DATE: / /

TODAY I AM THANKFUL FOR

A MOMENT TO REMEMBER

MY THOUGHTS ON TODAY

GOAL FOR TOMORROW

DATE: /   /

TODAY I AM THANKFUL FOR

A MOMENT TO REMEMBER

MY THOUGHTS ON TODAY

GOAL FOR TOMORROW

DATE: / /

TODAY I AM THANKFUL FOR

A MOMENT TO REMEMBER

MY THOUGHTS ON TODAY

GOAL FOR TOMORROW

DATE: / /

TODAY I AM THANKFUL FOR

A MOMENT TO REMEMBER

MY THOUGHTS ON TODAY

GOAL FOR TOMORROW

DATE: / /

TODAY I AM THANKFUL FOR

A MOMENT TO REMEMBER

MY THOUGHTS ON TODAY

GOAL FOR TOMORROW

DATE: / /

TODAY I AM THANKFUL FOR

A MOMENT TO REMEMBER

MY THOUGHTS ON TODAY

GOAL FOR TOMORROW

DATE: / /

---- TODAY I AM THANKFUL FOR ----

---- A MOMENT TO REMEMBER ----

---- MY THOUGHTS ON TODAY ----

---- GOAL FOR TOMORROW ----

DATE: /   /

TODAY I AM THANKFUL FOR

A MOMENT TO REMEMBER

MY THOUGHTS ON TODAY

GOAL FOR TOMORROW

DATE: / /

TODAY I AM THANKFUL FOR

A MOMENT TO REMEMBER

MY THOUGHTS ON TODAY

GOAL FOR TOMORROW

DATE: /   /

TODAY I AM THANKFUL FOR

A MOMENT TO REMEMBER

MY THOUGHTS ON TODAY

GOAL FOR TOMORROW

DATE: / /

TODAY I AM THANKFUL FOR

A MOMENT TO REMEMBER

MY THOUGHTS ON TODAY

GOAL FOR TOMORROW

DATE: /   /

TODAY I AM THANKFUL FOR

A MOMENT TO REMEMBER

MY THOUGHTS ON TODAY

GOAL FOR TOMORROW

DATE: / /

TODAY I AM THANKFUL FOR

A MOMENT TO REMEMBER

MY THOUGHTS ON TODAY

GOAL FOR TOMORROW

DATE: / /

TODAY I AM THANKFUL FOR

A MOMENT TO REMEMBER

MY THOUGHTS ON TODAY

GOAL FOR TOMORROW

DATE: /   /

TODAY I AM THANKFUL FOR

A MOMENT TO REMEMBER

MY THOUGHTS ON TODAY

GOAL FOR TOMORROW

DATE: / /

TODAY I AM THANKFUL FOR

A MOMENT TO REMEMBER

MY THOUGHTS ON TODAY

GOAL FOR TOMORROW

DATE: / /

TODAY I AM THANKFUL FOR

A MOMENT TO REMEMBER

MY THOUGHTS ON TODAY

GOAL FOR TOMORROW

DATE: / /

TODAY I AM THANKFUL FOR

A MOMENT TO REMEMBER

MY THOUGHTS ON TODAY

GOAL FOR TOMORROW

DATE: / /

TODAY I AM THANKFUL FOR

A MOMENT TO REMEMBER

MY THOUGHTS ON TODAY

GOAL FOR TOMORROW

DATE: /   /

TODAY I AM THANKFUL FOR

A MOMENT TO REMEMBER

MY THOUGHTS ON TODAY

GOAL FOR TOMORROW

DATE: / /

TODAY I AM THANKFUL FOR

A MOMENT TO REMEMBER

MY THOUGHTS ON TODAY

GOAL FOR TOMORROW

DATE: /   /

TODAY I AM THANKFUL FOR

A MOMENT TO REMEMBER

MY THOUGHTS ON TODAY

GOAL FOR TOMORROW

DATE: / /

TODAY I AM THANKFUL FOR

A MOMENT TO REMEMBER

MY THOUGHTS ON TODAY

GOAL FOR TOMORROW

DATE: / /

TODAY I AM THANKFUL FOR

A MOMENT TO REMEMBER

MY THOUGHTS ON TODAY

GOAL FOR TOMORROW

DATE: / /

TODAY I AM THANKFUL FOR

A MOMENT TO REMEMBER

MY THOUGHTS ON TODAY

GOAL FOR TOMORROW

DATE: / /

TODAY I AM THANKFUL FOR

A MOMENT TO REMEMBER

MY THOUGHTS ON TODAY

GOAL FOR TOMORROW

DATE: / /

TODAY I AM THANKFUL FOR

A MOMENT TO REMEMBER

MY THOUGHTS ON TODAY

GOAL FOR TOMORROW

DATE: / /

TODAY I AM THANKFUL FOR

A MOMENT TO REMEMBER

MY THOUGHTS ON TODAY

GOAL FOR TOMORROW

DATE: / /

TODAY I AM THANKFUL FOR

A MOMENT TO REMEMBER

MY THOUGHTS ON TODAY

GOAL FOR TOMORROW

DATE: / /

TODAY I AM THANKFUL FOR

A MOMENT TO REMEMBER

MY THOUGHTS ON TODAY

GOAL FOR TOMORROW

DATE: / /

TODAY I AM THANKFUL FOR

A MOMENT TO REMEMBER

MY THOUGHTS ON TODAY

GOAL FOR TOMORROW

DATE: / /

TODAY I AM THANKFUL FOR

A MOMENT TO REMEMBER

MY THOUGHTS ON TODAY

GOAL FOR TOMORROW

DATE: / /

TODAY I AM THANKFUL FOR

A MOMENT TO REMEMBER

MY THOUGHTS ON TODAY

GOAL FOR TOMORROW

DATE: / /

TODAY I AM THANKFUL FOR

A MOMENT TO REMEMBER

MY THOUGHTS ON TODAY

GOAL FOR TOMORROW

DATE: / /

TODAY I AM THANKFUL FOR

A MOMENT TO REMEMBER

MY THOUGHTS ON TODAY

GOAL FOR TOMORROW

DATE: / /

TODAY I AM THANKFUL FOR

A MOMENT TO REMEMBER

MY THOUGHTS ON TODAY

GOAL FOR TOMORROW

DATE: / /

TODAY I AM THANKFUL FOR

A MOMENT TO REMEMBER

MY THOUGHTS ON TODAY

GOAL FOR TOMORROW

DATE: / /

TODAY I AM THANKFUL FOR

A MOMENT TO REMEMBER

MY THOUGHTS ON TODAY

GOAL FOR TOMORROW

DATE: / /

TODAY I AM THANKFUL FOR

A MOMENT TO REMEMBER

MY THOUGHTS ON TODAY

GOAL FOR TOMORROW

DATE: / /

TODAY I AM THANKFUL FOR

A MOMENT TO REMEMBER

MY THOUGHTS ON TODAY

GOAL FOR TOMORROW

DATE: / /

TODAY I AM THANKFUL FOR

A MOMENT TO REMEMBER

MY THOUGHTS ON TODAY

GOAL FOR TOMORROW

DATE: / /

TODAY I AM THANKFUL FOR

A MOMENT TO REMEMBER

MY THOUGHTS ON TODAY

GOAL FOR TOMORROW

DATE: / /

TODAY I AM THANKFUL FOR

A MOMENT TO REMEMBER

MY THOUGHTS ON TODAY

GOAL FOR TOMORROW

DATE: / /

TODAY I AM THANKFUL FOR

A MOMENT TO REMEMBER

MY THOUGHTS ON TODAY

GOAL FOR TOMORROW

DATE: / /

TODAY I AM THANKFUL FOR

A MOMENT TO REMEMBER

MY THOUGHTS ON TODAY

GOAL FOR TOMORROW

DATE: / /

TODAY I AM THANKFUL FOR

A MOMENT TO REMEMBER

MY THOUGHTS ON TODAY

GOAL FOR TOMORROW

DATE: / /

TODAY I AM THANKFUL FOR

A MOMENT TO REMEMBER

MY THOUGHTS ON TODAY

GOAL FOR TOMORROW

DATE: /   /

TODAY I AM THANKFUL FOR

A MOMENT TO REMEMBER

MY THOUGHTS ON TODAY

GOAL FOR TOMORROW

DATE: / /

TODAY I AM THANKFUL FOR

A MOMENT TO REMEMBER

MY THOUGHTS ON TODAY

GOAL FOR TOMORROW

DATE: / /

TODAY I AM THANKFUL FOR

A MOMENT TO REMEMBER

MY THOUGHTS ON TODAY

GOAL FOR TOMORROW

DATE: / /

TODAY I AM THANKFUL FOR

A MOMENT TO REMEMBER

MY THOUGHTS ON TODAY

GOAL FOR TOMORROW

DATE: / /

TODAY I AM THANKFUL FOR

A MOMENT TO REMEMBER

MY THOUGHTS ON TODAY

GOAL FOR TOMORROW

DATE: / /

TODAY I AM THANKFUL FOR

A MOMENT TO REMEMBER

MY THOUGHTS ON TODAY

GOAL FOR TOMORROW

DATE: / /

TODAY I AM THANKFUL FOR

A MOMENT TO REMEMBER

MY THOUGHTS ON TODAY

GOAL FOR TOMORROW

DATE: / /

TODAY I AM THANKFUL FOR

A MOMENT TO REMEMBER

MY THOUGHTS ON TODAY

GOAL FOR TOMORROW

DATE: / /

TODAY I AM THANKFUL FOR

A MOMENT TO REMEMBER

MY THOUGHTS ON TODAY

GOAL FOR TOMORROW

DATE: / /

TODAY I AM THANKFUL FOR

A MOMENT TO REMEMBER

MY THOUGHTS ON TODAY

GOAL FOR TOMORROW

DATE: /   /

TODAY I AM THANKFUL FOR

A MOMENT TO REMEMBER

MY THOUGHTS ON TODAY

GOAL FOR TOMORROW

DATE: / /

TODAY I AM THANKFUL FOR

A MOMENT TO REMEMBER

MY THOUGHTS ON TODAY

GOAL FOR TOMORROW

DATE: / /

TODAY I AM THANKFUL FOR

A MOMENT TO REMEMBER

MY THOUGHTS ON TODAY

GOAL FOR TOMORROW

DATE: / /

TODAY I AM THANKFUL FOR

A MOMENT TO REMEMBER

MY THOUGHTS ON TODAY

GOAL FOR TOMORROW

DATE: / /

TODAY I AM THANKFUL FOR

A MOMENT TO REMEMBER

MY THOUGHTS ON TODAY

GOAL FOR TOMORROW

DATE: / /

TODAY I AM THANKFUL FOR

A MOMENT TO REMEMBER

MY THOUGHTS ON TODAY

GOAL FOR TOMORROW

DATE: / /

TODAY I AM THANKFUL FOR

A MOMENT TO REMEMBER

MY THOUGHTS ON TODAY

GOAL FOR TOMORROW

DATE: / /

TODAY I AM THANKFUL FOR

A MOMENT TO REMEMBER

MY THOUGHTS ON TODAY

GOAL FOR TOMORROW

DATE: / /

TODAY I AM THANKFUL FOR

A MOMENT TO REMEMBER

MY THOUGHTS ON TODAY

GOAL FOR TOMORROW

DATE: / /

TODAY I AM THANKFUL FOR

A MOMENT TO REMEMBER

MY THOUGHTS ON TODAY

GOAL FOR TOMORROW

DATE: / /

TODAY I AM THANKFUL FOR

A MOMENT TO REMEMBER

MY THOUGHTS ON TODAY

GOAL FOR TOMORROW

DATE: / /

TODAY I AM THANKFUL FOR

A MOMENT TO REMEMBER

MY THOUGHTS ON TODAY

GOAL FOR TOMORROW

DATE: / /

TODAY I AM THANKFUL FOR

A MOMENT TO REMEMBER

MY THOUGHTS ON TODAY

GOAL FOR TOMORROW

DATE: / /

TODAY I AM THANKFUL FOR

A MOMENT TO REMEMBER

MY THOUGHTS ON TODAY

GOAL FOR TOMORROW

DATE: /   /

TODAY I AM THANKFUL FOR

A MOMENT TO REMEMBER

MY THOUGHTS ON TODAY

GOAL FOR TOMORROW

DATE: / /

TODAY I AM THANKFUL FOR

A MOMENT TO REMEMBER

MY THOUGHTS ON TODAY

GOAL FOR TOMORROW

DATE: / /

TODAY I AM THANKFUL FOR

A MOMENT TO REMEMBER

MY THOUGHTS ON TODAY

GOAL FOR TOMORROW

DATE: / /

TODAY I AM THANKFUL FOR

A MOMENT TO REMEMBER

MY THOUGHTS ON TODAY

GOAL FOR TOMORROW

DATE: / /

TODAY I AM THANKFUL FOR

A MOMENT TO REMEMBER

MY THOUGHTS ON TODAY

GOAL FOR TOMORROW

DATE: / /

TODAY I AM THANKFUL FOR

A MOMENT TO REMEMBER

MY THOUGHTS ON TODAY

GOAL FOR TOMORROW

DATE: / /

TODAY I AM THANKFUL FOR

A MOMENT TO REMEMBER

MY THOUGHTS ON TODAY

GOAL FOR TOMORROW

DATE: / /

TODAY I AM THANKFUL FOR

A MOMENT TO REMEMBER

MY THOUGHTS ON TODAY

GOAL FOR TOMORROW

DATE: /   /

TODAY I AM THANKFUL FOR

A MOMENT TO REMEMBER

MY THOUGHTS ON TODAY

GOAL FOR TOMORROW

DATE: / /

TODAY I AM THANKFUL FOR

A MOMENT TO REMEMBER

MY THOUGHTS ON TODAY

GOAL FOR TOMORROW

DATE: / /

TODAY I AM THANKFUL FOR

A MOMENT TO REMEMBER

MY THOUGHTS ON TODAY

GOAL FOR TOMORROW

DATE: / /

TODAY I AM THANKFUL FOR

A MOMENT TO REMEMBER

MY THOUGHTS ON TODAY

GOAL FOR TOMORROW

DATE: / /

TODAY I AM THANKFUL FOR

A MOMENT TO REMEMBER

MY THOUGHTS ON TODAY

GOAL FOR TOMORROW

DATE: / /

TODAY I AM THANKFUL FOR

A MOMENT TO REMEMBER

MY THOUGHTS ON TODAY

GOAL FOR TOMORROW

DATE: / /

TODAY I AM THANKFUL FOR

A MOMENT TO REMEMBER

MY THOUGHTS ON TODAY

GOAL FOR TOMORROW

DATE: / /

TODAY I AM THANKFUL FOR

A MOMENT TO REMEMBER

MY THOUGHTS ON TODAY

GOAL FOR TOMORROW

DATE: / /

TODAY I AM THANKFUL FOR

A MOMENT TO REMEMBER

MY THOUGHTS ON TODAY

GOAL FOR TOMORROW

DATE: / /

TODAY I AM THANKFUL FOR

A MOMENT TO REMEMBER

MY THOUGHTS ON TODAY

GOAL FOR TOMORROW

DATE: / /

TODAY I AM THANKFUL FOR

A MOMENT TO REMEMBER

MY THOUGHTS ON TODAY

GOAL FOR TOMORROW

DATE: / /

TODAY I AM THANKFUL FOR

A MOMENT TO REMEMBER

MY THOUGHTS ON TODAY

GOAL FOR TOMORROW

DATE: /   /

TODAY I AM THANKFUL FOR

A MOMENT TO REMEMBER

MY THOUGHTS ON TODAY

GOAL FOR TOMORROW

DATE: /   /

TODAY I AM THANKFUL FOR

A MOMENT TO REMEMBER

MY THOUGHTS ON TODAY

GOAL FOR TOMORROW

DATE: / /

TODAY I AM THANKFUL FOR

A MOMENT TO REMEMBER

MY THOUGHTS ON TODAY

GOAL FOR TOMORROW

GRATITUDE CHANGES EVERYTHING

Made in the USA
Monee, IL
26 November 2022